D0068216

REFERRAL UPGRADE

"Just read Hank's book for the third time, gave it out to a number of my associates and received great feedback on its unique ideas!!! Hearing from a top producer on referrals, and not a consultant, lends a ton of credibility to his words. Thanks, Hank, for giving back."

ROBERT E. WALKER, CLU, CHFC

CEO of Wealth Cornerstones, General Agent, Ohio National

"If you want to live your dreams, one of the best ways to do that is to help others to live theirs. This beautiful book will show you how you can do that every day, and find your very best clients in the process."

MARY MORRISSEY,

Speaker, bestselling author and founder of LifeSOULutions

"As Hank Frazee says in his book, Referral Upgrade, *'referrals are the lifeblood of any successful business.' In the book, Hank gives us a unique methodology that will earn us more referrals by utilizing the most effective means of initiating a business or strategic relationship. The wisdom in these pages offers insight into the giving mindset that is necessary in any healthy relationship. If one of your goals for your business is to experience growth through referrals and key relationships, this book was written for you. Thanks, Hank!"*

MICHAEL J. ANDRADA

Financial Consultant, AXA Advisors, Retirement Benefits Group

"Referrals are currency in business, an asset that very few people utilize strategically. From the moment you start reading this book, you'll discover a simple process that can transform the way you get clients to come to you, and you'll have the capability to reach your very best opportunities and relationships. This will help you truly develop an E.L.F.™ business (Easy, Lucrative and Fun™)."

JOE POLISH,

President and Founder, Genius Network and www.ILoveMarketing.com

"In Referral Upgrade, *Hank Frazee gives us a refreshing, effective, practical way to upgrade our referred lead prospecting.*

After describing the inherent weakness of the traditional method of obtaining referrals, Hank takes us on the journey which evolved into a system where people actually want to give referrals. Hank's method is revolutionary because it requires an attitude shift for the sales person. On the other hand, it's very practical because Hank outlines a step-by-step process to get the referrals you want and deserve. Hank's phenomenal success is proof that his method works.

Throughout the book, you cannot escape Hank's attitude toward people, in general, and business, in particular. As Hank says in his chapter on persistence, 'We are here to help one another.'"

MARK BUGLI, CLU, CHFC

Director of Advanced Life Marketing
Total Financial & Insurance Services, Inc.

"It has been truly a pleasure reading this book! Thank you so much, Hank, for helping to illustrate the right perspective for a young upstart getting into the business. God bless."

BART BURSON,

Life Insurance Agent

"Hank Frazee gets it! He has done the heavy lifting for all of us who depend on new prospects to grow our businesses. Read this book, and you'll heat up your business and get real results."

ROYCE IMHOFF,

Business Development, Lion Street, Inc.

"In Referral Upgrade, Hank Frazee changes the game by providing a powerful new framework to teach salespeople everywhere how to spend their time in front of their best customers. A crucial new addition to the discussion of the art of the sale."

DAN SULLIVAN,

President and Founder of Strategic Coach®

"I've read lots of books on referrals. Hank's book is different...[He] lays out strategies that encourage other advisors to want to refer you. In my 48 years in this business, this is one of the best books I've read on this subject. Try Hank's approach. It works."

GENE MAHN, CLU, CHFC

MDRT Past President

REFERRAL
UPGRADE

A New Way to Find Your Very Best Clients

HANK FRAZEE

HankFrazee.com

Sycamore Canyon Publishing, LLC

Calabasas, California

REFERRAL UPGRADE

A New Way to Find Your Very Best Clients

By Hank Frazee

Published by
Sycamore Canyon Publishing, LLC

Copyright © 2014 by Hank Frazee

ISBN: 978-0-9843511-3-8

Library of Congress Control Number: Pending

Book cover and interior design by Peri Poloni-Gabriel, Knockout Design, www.knockoutbooks.com.

Edited by Elizabeth Frazee, Elizabeth@sycamorecanyonpublishing.com.

Printed in the United States of America

ALSO BY HANK FRAZEE

*Before We Say
"Goodnight"*

How to Tell Bedtime Stories About
Your Life and Family

Contents

To my Dad, Harry,
for teaching me the value of integrity,
loyalty and hard work.

———∞∞∞———

To my Mother, Mary,
for always encouraging me and believing
in my ever evolving vision.

Is this Book for You?

NEARLY ALL OF YOUR BEST CLIENTS and referral sources have a vision of their best life going forward. *Referral Upgrade* will teach you a simple method to discover and understand their vision and who and what can bring that vision to life. You can help your best contacts make their vision a reality by introducing them to their Big Three—their very best clients, referral sources and opportunities. They, in turn, will want to do the same for you, so that you can attain and live the life of your dreams.

The ideas and methods proposed here are based on my thirty-plus years experience in the financial services industry. I use them daily to introduce my clients and referral sources to the people and ideas that can help them live their dreams. This is the shortest possible route to their success and yours. When you do this for others, a metamorphosis occurs, and they see you in a completely different light. They see you as an incredible resource in the attainment of their dreams, and they will want to refer you too.

This process is for anyone providing products and services to clients, and particularly for those who want to meet more of their Big Three. I will show you how to meet as many of your ideal clients and referral sources as you would like and how to build those introductions to be mutually rewarding relationships for everyone concerned. How is that possible, you may wonder. Read this book and find out. It has worked for everyone with whom I've shared this, and it can work for you too.

AUTHOR'S NOTE

WHEN YOU SEE REFERENCES TO "best clients," "referral sources," "referrers" or "opportunities," I mean the very best in each category. These are the people with whom you love to work.

The terms "referral sources" and "referrers" are used interchangeably in the book and mean any of three types of people who introduce you to your very best clients. They can be:

✧ A STRATEGIC PARTNER—*someone in your industry with whom you share revenue and who refers you to your Big Three.*

✧ A CENTER OF INFLUENCE—*someone in a related industry with whom you don't share revenue but who refers you to your Big Three.*

✧ A FRIEND—*anyone who can introduce you to your Big Three.*

In the interest of simplicity, masculine and feminine pronouns are used interchangeably.

"Give and you will receive."

LUKE 6:38

⸺⸺

INTRODUCTION

T HANK YOU FOR READING THIS BOOK. It will lead you to your very best clients in numbers that you never dreamed possible. On the pathway of that journey lies a challenge you likely face and a promise I will make.

THE CHALLENGE:

✧ *Good referrals to the right client are the lifeblood of any business and can be a struggle to obtain.*

THE PROMISE:

✧ *Your opportunity to be referred over and over again to your very best clients has never been better.*

This book will show you how to make this promise your own personal reality. You will learn how to dramatically increase your access to your best opportunities and how you can begin to put your plan into action today.

Do a good job and market well within your existing client base, and you will be referred. The old-school method of asking for referrals works, but *Referral Upgrade* works better. It can lead to greater success by teaching you a unique method to find your very best clients by introducing others to theirs. This is incredibly effective at getting the referrals of your dreams often without even asking for them. Based on my experience and those I've shared this method with, it works. And it will work for you too, because the magic is in the message rather than the messenger.

Though easy and fun, this method will work only if you apply it. You may get results from your very first interview, though this is really an ongoing process. It is a shift in mindset and behavior that will create a steady stream of introductions to your best opportunities. Your relationships with your best clients and referrers are about to get a whole lot better.

1

Referral Upgrade

*"We are often faced with
great opportunities brilliantly disguised
as unsolvable problems."*

Lee Iacocca

As I see it, my job is to help people achieve their dreams. It's that simple. I connect the right people to the right people or ideas. When I do that, everything works out well, for them and for me. The more clients I help in this way and the bigger the numbers, the better the results. Your business likely works in a similar way.

But what about referrals? Are you being referred randomly to just anyone, or are you being referred steadily to your very best clients? It's time to trade too few referrals to just anyone for as many referrals as you'd like to just the right people for you.

Asking for referrals in the usual way can feel like flying standby. When you're flying standby, you have no idea if you'll make your flight or where you will be sitting. It's a random proposition, as is the old-school way of asking for referrals. Ever used a phrase like, "Whom do you know that I might be able to help in the same way I've helped you?" How well does that work? You can continue to fly standby and receive the occasional referral, or apply the ideas in this book and get a lifetime of referral upgrades, and you can start today.

Referrals are regarded as the gold standard for business development for good reason. They are the gold standard. Referrals are currency in business. They are an asset and turn into real money. And money is the by-product of the service you provide for others. The right referral can make your year, or even your career.

I know what it feels like to miss your shot at your dream referral. It hurts you and your family and the people you serve too, because they need what you provide, and so do their friends. I know this because I have spent over thirty years in the life insurance business and worked my way from the ground up selling a product that most people don't want to buy and mistakenly think they have to die to benefit from.

The trouble is that asking for referrals is literally like asking your clients to give you a gift that can harm them and annoy their friends. It's natural to feel you have earned that gift if you have done an exceptional job. But asking them to refer you on the premise of helping their friends can sound to them like, "Give me a gift, so I can sell your friends too." That's often the way other people hear it, and it puts them in an awkward position. Though they may like you personally, they're afraid you may hurt their relationships and disrupt their income in the process.

Ever hear this reply to your request? "I can't think of anyone right now, but I'll keep it in mind." How many of those people call later with a referral? Picture yourself in a typical sales interview at the moment you ask for referrals. If you could read their thoughts, you might hear the following questions:

✧ *Can I trust you enough to refer you to my best contacts, whom I have spent years developing?*

✧ *Will you hurt my relationship with them?*

✧ *Will you refer me?*

When this happens, you're right back to flying standby on a plane bound for nowhere. Furthermore, since they don't have any idea who your Big Three—your ideal client, ideal advisor and ideal opportunities—are, how can they refer you to them? Do you want proof that the above statements are true? Consider for a moment how you feel and respond when others ask you to refer them.

Instead, let's imagine the following scenarios:

✧ *What if there was a way to meet people who actually want to refer you to your Big Three and even volunteer to do so?*

✧ *What if you had a method to significantly increase their confidence in you and reduce their risk of referring you?*

✧ *What if they thought it was more valuable to refer you, rather than your competitor, to their best clients and other contacts?*

At this point, you may be thinking this sounds great but way too good to be true. It is true, and I will show you exactly how to make this happen over and over again and how to build a team of rainmakers eager to refer you. This is a process that turns getting referrals on its head, while making it fun and exciting for you and your referrer.

Let me give you two real-life examples. In the first, I used these principles unconsciously, while, in the second, I used them intentionally.

About twenty years ago, I invited the president of a local business group to lunch, as I was interested in joining her organization to promote a joint venture with a life insurance company and the U.S. Chamber of Commerce on a national quality award for small businesses. It was called "The Blue Chip Enterprise Initiative," and I had no idea the amazing results and insights it would lead to. Having asked whom she could recommend in her organization that I might interview, she gave me 25 names. I went to see them one by one. Now this was long before I thought of the ideas described here, but there are some important similarities.

The first prospect on the list, Rick, was a successful manufacturer. I told him what I did for a living and that he had been recommended as a candidate for the U.S. Chamber Small Business Quality Award. Keep in mind that I was simply trying to meet business owners on good terms that might someday turn into clients. He was clearly touched that he had been recommended by the president of his business organization, but said, "We like to keep our ideas quiet, but can you sell me $5,000,000 of life insurance?" I gulped, said yes and ended up selling him $28,000,000 of insurance, over the next several years, which turned out to be the amount he ultimately wanted. At the time, it was the biggest sale of my career.

More recently, I told a friend of mine about this process, and he suggested I go see his friend, John. He said John was well connected and was president of a sailing club, implying that the members of that club might be good prospects for me as well. I called John, and he invited me to come to his office. During the interview, he told me that he was expanding his company and asked if I could sell him $20,000,000 of life insurance.

Here's the point: I wasn't trying to sell insurance to either Rick or John, yet in both cases they initiated the purchase. This just happens when you interview people and focus on them, and I don't think it really matters what kind of interview it is. Come from the place of "How can I help you get where you want to go?" Listen and give them your complete attention and time. You want to hear their story. It's focusing on them and un-derstanding their vision, without trying to sell anything, which makes the magic happen.

Most people have no idea how to do this and will keep flying standby. Worse yet, some readers may skim through this and say, "Oh yeah, I get it, don't try to sell them," but they will miss the point and the opportunity. *Referral Upgrade* works, and it will work for you too. I've made all the mistakes before you and will show you how to stay on track and win. The wonderful news is that you can go back to all your clients who didn't refer you the first time and, using these methods, get great referrals now.

Until I discovered this process, I searched diligently for ways to ask for referrals. I attended lectures, read books and articles, and it all boiled down to two things: exceed your client's expectations and ask for referrals. Good idea, but this is better. Give it a try, and you will develop a deeper collaborative relationship with your ideal clients and referrers and create a lifetime of access to your best opportunities. It will blow your previous results out of the water. So stop flying standby, turn the page and begin a lifetime of referral upgrades.

2

STICK WITH IT

*"It was impossible...so it took us a little longer
than we thought it would."*

WALLY BYUM

MOST OF MY BUSINESS DAYS ARE spent in
meetings or on the phone with my best clients
and referral sources and at events and places where they
gather. This is by design, though it wasn't always this
way. On the day I said yes to the life insurance business,
both the manager and assistant manager of our agency
quit. Was it something I said? Was it my beard? For my
first six months in the business, I sold no policies, not
counting the health insurance policy I sold to my sister,
though I called day and night. Nothing worked, but I
kept trying and working that phone every day.

I called every group of professionals conceivable, architects, physicians, accountants, lawyers, contractors, chiropractors, dentists. Something finally clicked with the dentists, and a little success with them continued to grow. When I did sell my first life insurance policy in the seventh month, the commission was $12.50 paid monthly.

After years of grinding it out, and with the help of many mentors and seminars, I began working with bigger clients. But still, I felt awkward. I told myself I didn't know enough and didn't have enough experience to match my imaginary competition. I call this "the pretty girl syndrome." Much like in high school and afraid to walk across the gym to ask the girls to dance, I hesitated to ask the big prospects for appointments. What if they said no? What if they said yes? If you suffer from this condition, do joint work with someone more experienced than you and split the case. You will learn and make money as you grow, and you will quit wasting energy kicking yourself.

Eventually, I worked up to over 300 dentist clients, as a result of persistent effort and another referral technique

I invented that was very simple and worked nearly every time. I created a list of several thousand dentists in the Los Angeles area. When delivering an approved policy, I pulled out the list and, handing it to the dentist, said these exact words, "What I've asked a lot of my dentist clients to do is to check off who they know that I might send a letter to." That was my referral speech in its entirety, and I never varied from it. I noticed that if they took the list, they always checked off names of the dentists they knew right then and gave it back to me. As they handed it back, I asked, "May I say you suggested I call?" The answer was always yes, and I never received less than 15 referrals. My best was over 400 referrals in one visit from a dentist who had a heart attack shortly after I had sold him a disability insurance policy. Afterwards, he was so grateful to have the policy that he did everything he could to help me succeed. If you have access to a list of a group of interrelated people that you would like to work with, you might try this. A word of caution, use this method only where you are authorized to use such a list for business purposes.

I began in life insurance knowing nothing and no one and was as green as they get. Just like thousands of others, I struggled, barely making it through my first year in the business. I had no idea how to sell insurance or how to find a client. But I "stuck with it," the three magic words to success in anything, and gradually rose to the Top of The Table—the top one percent of life insurance agents internationally.

Not long ago, in an estate planning case with my partners, our new client asked his accountant and attorney to review our recommendation. After some discussion, the attorney called our plan, "Brilliant!" In a subsequent conversation, our client told us, "If you can get these two guys, they have the wealthiest clients in the city." We dreamed of the day when, after asking the advisors for referrals, they would introduce us to all of their top clients. After all, they considered our ideas brilliant, and they were. Having completed the case, we went to see both advisors in separate interviews and gave them our referral pitch, and both told us in nearly identical terms that they would definitely keep us in mind if something came up. That was fun, and we are still waiting.

Have you had this experience? You have a brilliant idea. They love it, they do it, but they don't refer you. Why is that? Because they are afraid. The old way of asking for referrals plugs right into their fear that you will somehow mismanage the relationship. It can be a painful experience for them and for you. Simply put, this book will show you how to calm those fears and discover their vision, which will lead to winning relationships on all sides.

Just like you, I was flying standby when asking for referrals until I had an "aha moment" that woke me up in the middle of the night. Suddenly it occurred to me, "What if I just focused on referring them?" As I kept turning the question over in my mind, I resolved to help others reach their dreams by introducing them to those who could help them get there. That insight gradually led to this book.

The next day, I had lunch with an attorney who mentioned his good friend Paul who worked just on large real estate transactions. Paul had several heads of major corporations as clients, and it sounded like he really knew his stuff. I told the attorney I would like to meet Paul, since I knew someone he might be able to help with a hundred-million-plus real-estate portfolio.

Paul called me that afternoon, and we agreed to have lunch. If you were a real estate specialist and were told someone wanted to introduce you to such a client, how would you respond? I knew he would call me.

I must admit, in the back of my mind, I was thinking this introduction might lead to business for us. But my primary intention was just to help these individuals to meet. Remember, this was the first time I scheduled a meeting specifically thinking, what if I just focus on referring him? I was winging it and just playing around with the idea.

Paul asked me about my business, to which I gave a five-minute description of the value we provide our high-net-worth clients. Then I turned the tables and decided to practice the *Referral Upgrade* process for the first time. Rather than the usual back and forth conversation focused on me and my work, I just interviewed him about his dreams and whom he would like to meet.

We quickly developed rapport, and I soon learned more about him and his life dreams than I ever could during a typical business lunch. Towards the end of the interview, he said completely out of the blue, "Hey, I have four people that you should meet." Three of the four were my ideal client type. All four were his clients, which meant they would meet with me on his introduction.

The same thing happened *the next nine times* I used this process. On the tenth time, the interviewee said he wasn't looking to meet anyone but referred us anyhow, again, without being asked.

In hindsight, I noticed that their interest diminished when I talked about myself or drifted into conversation rather than staying in the interview mode. Just interview them. I'm sure you have witnessed this phenomenon in your life. A person who is genuinely interested in others can draw people out, and they glow with the attention. This works because such individuals are sincerely interested in others and are essentially interviewing them.

People rarely get such undivided attention, and they will come alive when they get it from you.

There is no better way to create and enhance rapport. Remember to focus on them, their vision and on referring them, and it will change your life.

3

THE WHOLE NINE YARDS

*"A pessimist sees the difficulty
in every opportunity; an optimist sees the
opportunity in every difficulty."*

WINSTON CHURCHILL

THIS CHAPTER WILL GIVE YOU A complete overview of the *Referral Upgrade* process, step by step. The solution to being referred to your best clients, referral sources and opportunities is to focus on helping your clients and referrers identify their vision and their Big Three.

Please note that this process is purposely focused on making introductions as the quickest methods of achieving your goals. What follows, then, is a brief review of each chapter.

Chapter 4: GIVING OPPORTUNITY

You must have a sincere desire to help others for this process to work. This doesn't need to be overcomplicated. Simply be genuine, stay with a giving mindset and follow through with appropriate action when you discover a way to help them. Your genuine interest in them and their vision is the first key to success in this system. The ideal referral is the one you give. Help your clients and referrers by identifying and introducing them to their Big Three, and they will introduce you to yours.

Chapter 5: THE SCREEN TESTS

Aim at working only with people that you like, trust and respect. If you like, trust and respect them, it is likely that they will like, trust, and respect you. And if they don't, they will never refer you.

In other words, work only with people you want to work with. That might include people who can introduce you to your Big Three, or anyone you would like to help, people who charge your batteries, regardless of whether they can lead you to your Big Three. Either way, helping others will help you to reach your goals, directly and indirectly.

Creating access to opportunity for the people you introduce will inspire and speed your progress. Often those opportunities come in social, business or civic groups where Big Threes congregate.

Chapter 6: YOUR BIG THREE

In this chapter, we will identify your Big Three. If you don't know what you're aiming at, you can't hit it. We will go through a question-and-answer process to identify your best clients, referral sources and opportunities. You'll gain confidence knowing exactly whom it is that you want to meet, specifically and by category.

Chapter 7: OBSTACLES AND SOLUTIONS

Let's face it. Our biggest obstacle is sitting on our shoulders right now. You may be having thoughts such as:

✧ *I can't do it.*

✧ *I don't have the expertise to have my dream client become, well, my client.*

✧ *I don't know anyone, or, the people I know don't know anyone.*

You can overcome all of this fairly easily, and we will address how to do so in Chapter 7.

Chapter 8: GET THE APPOINTMENT

Scheduling appointments can be challenging, time-consuming and tedious. We'll review two methods that can be used in person, by phone, email or even via text, by you or your assistant, to easily get you in front of your ideal client or referrer.

Chapter 9: THE BIG-THREE INTERVIEW

This is the second key to meeting your Big Three and the heart of this process. You will be interviewing your client or referrer, rather than having a conversation with him. And when you make it about him, it works beautifully.

Chapter 10: THE BIG-THREE PROFILE

The Big-Three interview is conducted using the Big-Three profile. It is designed to uncover information that will help you to introduce your client or referrer to people and ideas that will help him achieve his dreams. You will discover what your client or referrer hopes to achieve and whom he needs to meet to reach his goals.

Chapter 11: FOLLOW THROUGH

The third essential step is the follow through. If you miss this part of the process, you are squandering the good work done in the interview. This is where you show your client or referrer that you are someone he can depend on by doing what you say you're going to do. He will quickly recognize that you can be of extraordinary value to his realizing his dream.

This is your opportunity to prove yourself and earn his or her commitment to you. This is also a place where it is easy to drop the ball and tarnish your image. We will review how to prevent that.

Chapter 12: YOUR TEAM OF RAINMAKERS

As you progress in helping others using this system, you will see that many of the people you refer will truly resonate with you and will begin to refer you. Some will become your team of rainmakers, and they will refer you over and over again to your Big Three. You can achieve exponential results when you introduce your team of rainmakers to one another, creating a bond with them that will benefit all of you and your clients. This chapter will show you some easy ways to create and build your team and how to continually increase the quality of your introductions to each of your respective Big Threes.

There you have it. This book is meant to be practical, transferable and immediately applicable, and it can change your business and personal life for the better. So come out of the standby line. You have an upgrade, and we are about to take off!

4

GIVING OPPORTUNITY

"The measure of any man's life is the
impact he has on others."

ROBERTO CLEMENTE

Y OU MUST HAVE A GENUINE INTEREST in helping others for these concepts to work. This is key
and the most important point for your success with this
process. The ideal referral is the one you give to others,
though this is easily overlooked due to our tendency to
focus on ourselves. I am just as susceptible to this as
anyone. The challenge is to bring your best self to the
game, to be a champion for others. Connect your clients
and referrers with like-minded people who are looking
for them. Become a great resource, help them achieve
their dreams. You will transform your relationship with

everyone you meet, and their experience of you will rise to a new level.

Let me give you an example. A while back, I went to pitch a new idea to an advisor whom I have known for some time. About to begin my sales presentation, I suddenly thought, what am I doing, and switched to interview mode. This advisor had never referred me, though I had pitched ideas to him numerous times. What were the chances that he would refer me this time, if I simply pitched again? The interview took about an hour, and in the end I made a simple suggestion about how he could solve a logistical issue through one of my partners. That was it. Six months later, he introduced us to a billionaire client.

Giving makes you feel good, and your gift often benefits many others beyond the initial receiver of the gift. We can derive a great sense of purpose and meaning through giving, and it makes us better people in the process.

Writing this book has made me keenly aware of the immeasurable rewards of giving. You will find opportunities that were there all along, but you become aware of them only as a result of giving. Your chances of enjoying these benefits increase by focusing on others and their vision.

Here's another brief example. The other day, after doing a simple favor for a business advisor, he suggested that I could use my first book, *Before We Say "Goodnight:" How to tell bedtime stories about your life and family*, to connect with my Big Three. That tip later inspired another idea, which then inspired another. It is a certainty that none of these ideas would have occurred to me without my friend's suggestion, which was prompted by my doing a small favor for him. Over and over, you will discover that giving attracts opportunity.

You don't need to wait to interview your clients and referrers to introduce and connect them to their Big Three. You will find opportunities during the course of every day. What you practice becomes habitual and permanent, and you will continue to improve on it. It charges my batteries to introduce others to those who can help them achieve their dreams, and doing so has shortened the path to achieving mine, often in ways that I never anticipated.

5

THE SCREEN TESTS

"Regardless of the numbers, I never work with anyone I don't like, trust and respect."

WARREN BUFFET

THIS CHAPTER IS ABOUT POSITIONING YOURSELF to hit the ball out of the park and to enjoy yourself while you're at it. The screen tests described below are an easy way to help you identify the best people and opportunities for you. The beautiful thing is that the answers and insights you come up with will be unique to you and will lead you to the people you want to work with and to your best opportunities.

THE BUFFET TEST

When I first read Warren Buffet's quotation above, I realized that I had been putting up with a lot of baloney for a long time in order to make money. And yes, sometimes we have to. But you can choose to work mainly with people you enjoy and introduce them to others they will enjoy meeting as well. The Buffet test, as I began to call it, became my filter to screen out relationships that were not a good fit for me. Shifting my time and enthusiasm towards people I like, trust and respect is exponentially more rewarding and valuable to me and to everyone with whom I work. It is one of my core business practices and a great stress-reducer.

When I first put it into practice, only two of my clients did not pass the Buffet test in all three categories. I gradually moved them to agents for whom they might be a better fit. That freed up my time and energy to work with the people I really enjoyed. My staff liked this also, as those same people were hard on them too.

You know, Warren Buffet didn't make this up in some ivory tower while eating bon bons and watching *I Love Lucy* reruns. He provides immense value, leadership and inspiration to millions of people around the world. And he is one of the most charitable men in history. I imagine that he gradually realized that life was easier and more fun when he chose to work just with people he liked, trusted and respected. And if it's good enough for Warren, it's good enough for me.

I have discussed this test with many of my clients and friends, and they all love it. I've asked them never to introduce me to anyone they don't like, trust and respect, because if they don't like, trust and respect them, I won't either.

It took a little courage to say that the first time. But people respond positively to it for several reasons. First, they take it as a compliment, because it's obvious that I like, trust and respect them. I wouldn't be working with them otherwise, and they in turn work with me for the same reasons. It gives us a common language and standard to operate from.

From time to time, I hear one of my partners say, "This guy doesn't pass the Buffet test." As a result, we have turned away some very wealthy prospects. Though we do have one or two clients that can be challenging occasionally, this has made a marked difference in our enjoyment of our work on a daily basis. Now we apply the Buffet test to every relationship and opportunity we have. Working with people you genuinely enjoy will have a big impact on your success in business and overall happiness.

THE BATTERY TEST

Have you ever noticed that the days are too short to accomplish all the things that really matter to you? Or that much of the work you spend your time on is either boring or you're not particularly good at it? Would you like a simple method to clear out the things you don't like doing? I stumbled upon this concept in a brief conversation years ago.

While at a Strategic Coach® workshop, led by Dan Sullivan, I sat next to Harry, a man I'd never seen before or since, yet he had an immediate and permanent impact on me. Harry told me that he was going to retire in order to have more time to fish. Harry said, "You can't fish on a schedule." He had developed a simple test for how he spent his time, and it was this: "If it charges my batteries, I do it, and if it drains 'em, I don't."

That hit me like a lightning bolt. I thought of so many things that drained my batteries instead of charging them. Upon my return to work, I promptly resigned from three boards and delegated or deleted anything in my office that was not a good use of my time.

Thinking back on it, I was on those boards for reasons that did not advance the worthy causes they represented. I was there solely for business contacts, the wrong motive to be on any board. Join a board or volunteer for causes that charge your batteries, and give it your all.

Even worthwhile endeavors can drain your batteries when you are tired or stressed out. We all have personal obligations. Doing the dishes or going to a school meeting on a Tuesday night after a long workday isn't necessarily fun, but I choose to do those things because they are part of the larger meaning and purpose in my life. And that charges my batteries.

THE ACCESS-TO-OPPORTUNITY TEST

How would you like to greatly expand your chances of being referred every day to your Big Three? So far, we've identified having a giving mindset, conducting interviews and introducing others to their Big Three as the primary steps towards your ideal client. There is another way to daily deepen your connection to your Big Three.

One of my mentors, Denis Mullane, said to me years ago, "By and large, the people we do business with will be a cross-section of those we spend our time with." So if your Big Three spend their time together in certain groups and you join those groups, won't you do more business with them? You want to apply the Buffet and battery tests here as well. Is this the best group of its kind for you, and does it fit into your life and schedule?

Some years ago, my wife and I attended a charity dinner and were seated at the table of a new friend I met while serving on another charity board. We happened to be sitting near a walkway where dinner guests passed by throughout the evening. It just so happened that I knew many of those passing by, and we greeted each other as they walked by. My new friend noticed over the course of the dinner that I seemed to know just about everyone there. I really did not, but it appeared so to him.

Quite out of the blue, he suggested that I would make a great addition to an exclusive business group he belonged to and offered to propose me for membership. Though flattered, I just laughed it off. The next day, I mentioned the conversation to my friend Mike Whitmore. He quickly recognized it as a big opportunity and suggested that I give it some thought. As the idea grew on me, I decided to ask another good friend and mentor, Bill Hawkins, what he thought of it. He responded with these exact words, "Well, let me see, I think I would make that my number one, two and three priority."

This is the beauty of volunteering for charities that hold meaning for you. Be active in a charity you believe in, and great things will happen for you and for them. I was in the right place at the right time, somewhat by design, and was friendly to the people walking by our table at dinner. That gradually led to many friendships and a terrific source of ongoing opportunity.

You can build your own perpetual connectivity machine with a little thought and a plan. Look for an environment where your Big Three work, play, learn or give in abundance. The opportunities that flow from that will take you in the right direction while you are doing something you love.

Allow me to share some tips that can greatly increase your connectivity in any group:

✧ *Learn and remember the names of the people in your group and their significant others, if appropriate. Refer to the list of members before you go to an event, if you find that helpful.*

✧ *Make eye contact and greet them by name when you arrive and when you leave. Be engaging with others while you are there.*

✧ *Introduce yourself to new members and introduce them to others.*

✧ *Go out of your way to be friendly with members of the group who seem to need a little help connecting with others.*

✧ *Be more interested than interesting.*

✧ *Treat the staff well.*

Follow any of these suggestions, and you will more deeply connect with others.

"The eye sees only what the mind is ready to comprehend," wrote Canadian novelist Robertson Davies. Initially, I laughed off the idea of joining the business group when my friend suggested it, having never considered it. Looking back, however, joining that group was a major turning point in my career. I've gradually realized that one of the quickest ways to the life of your dreams is to make the most of today's opportunities.

6

YOUR BIG THREE

*"The only difference between big
and small is the size."*

A SIGN ON THE WALL AT
KING'S FISH HOUSE

W E HAVE ONLY SO MUCH TIME in each day. So let's invest it in the most satisfying and profitable way we can, for ourselves and for others. Doesn't it make sense to go after our best opportunities? Yet if we don't know specifically whom we want to meet, how can we expect our clients and referral sources to know?

It's fine if your idea of your Big Three is a bit vague right now. You may not have considered these questions before, but you will want to know exactly who they are before you conduct your first Big-Three interview. By the end of this chapter, you'll have the opportunity to answer some questions that will give you greater clarity about your Big Three.

Most of us ask to be referred to, well, anyone. But you don't want to be referred to just anyone. You want to be referred to your best possible clients and referral sources. You might be more specific and ask, "Whom do you know that I can help in this kind of work?" It's likely that even then you will get a pretty vague answer. You are asking your client to determine who is a good match for your product or service without clear direction from you.

You want your potential referrer to know exactly who your ideal client is and precisely how your product or service can benefit him. And you want to know the same information about the person you are interviewing. And only he can answer the question, "Whom do I want to work with, who are my best referral sources and what are my best opportunities?" It is highly probable he will not have given this much thought either, until you ask him. Let's consider the Big Three one at a time.

YOUR BEST CLIENTS

Is he or she single, married or have a family? How old is he or she? Is marital status or age relevant to your business? Does he or she own a business? Is your best client the business itself, the business owner, the executives or the staff? I tend to think of my best client as the person who writes the check or has the power to say yes to what I am offering.

Do you want to go after the biggest clients you can find, or is mom-and-pop your battery charging market? Is your market wealthy families, athletes, a specific type of business, charities, or someone else entirely?

You can have more than one type of best client, but if you have too many, perhaps you need to be more focused. Get as specific as you can in identifying your best clients and come up with a detailed written statement of who they are. Provide details so that you and your referrer will know them when you see them. See the example of my Big Three.

Your Best Referral Sources

Referrers are individuals who have a relationship of trust with your Big Three, either as friends or advisors. Chances are your Big Three are quite similar to those of your best referrers. For example, you and your referrers may have working relationships with attorneys, accountants or bankers. Or, perhaps, your best referrers work in the same or a related industry, but in a different business or a subset of your business.

Access to Your Best Opportunities

This is a broad category because opportunity is in the eye of the beholder. Opportunities represent people, places and things that attract your best clients and referral sources, such as membership in a particular social or business organization. You want a group that passes your screen tests and attracts plenty of your best clients and referral sources.

Are your best opportunities found in civic or business groups or perhaps golf or car clubs? Is it the Chevy Club or the Lamborghini Club? Opportunities can be found during one-on-one or smaller-group experiences.

A good opportunity doesn't have to be elaborate. Having someone over or out for dinner with his or her family are good examples. Use your imagination and create your own specific opportunities, such as events and gatherings of almost any kind, anywhere.

To give another example, recently I was privileged to participate in creating both a golf group and a business group of about forty people each. Both groups evolved from unexpected conversations while playing golf and at lunch with colleagues and friends. These turned out to be great opportunities for everyone involved. Give yourself access to opportunity through your membership in groups that attract your Big Three and watch the magic happen.

Opportunities are often indirectly beneficial. To paraphrase Robert Louis Stevenson, "Judge each day not just by the harvest you reap, but by the seeds you plant." The briefest of conversations or encounters can lead to wonderful opportunities.

Often, I will attend an event or meet with someone, and what I thought was the opportunity in fact pales by comparison with the much bigger opportunity that eventually unfolds. Take, for instance, the day I attended a continuing education seminar with my friend Eric Miner, who eventually introduced me to my wife. That was a terrific day. My kids think so too.

MY BIG THREE

Below is a detailed description of my Big Three to help spark your thinking. My Big Three have changed dramatically over the years and continue to change as my ideas, opportunities and business evolve.

My Best Clients

I have three distinct best-client categories:

Individuals and Families

They are intelligent, usually married, with children and perhaps grandchildren. They love their family. They are charitably involved and civically and socially active. They have a high-net worth and are insurable.

They pass my screen tests. They are concerned about how their children will turn out, about their personal and family legacy and estate taxes. In a perfect world, they are connected to other Big Threes. They have dreams they want to fulfill and are looking for opportunity. That gives me an opening to introduce them to people and ideas that can help them realize their vision. Many of the opportunities I might share with them have nothing to do with insurance.

It should be easy to support your criteria for selecting your ideal client. Ask yourself why he or she would have these characteristics. For example, the reason my ideal client is usually married or has children is because no one buys life insurance if he or she doesn't love someone or something, such as his or her family or a charitable cause.

Charities

Successful charities with a committed donor base. We have expertise that can greatly increase the success and certainty of their fundraising.

Businesses

Successful businesses with net annual revenue over one hundred million dollars are the third category of ideal client for our team. We have solutions for businesses of this size and caliber that can supercharge their success and increase their security.

My Ideal Referral Sources

Our preferred referral sources work with our best client type, as a regular part of their business. These advisors are educated about and/or are open to learning more about high net-worth wealth transfer or charitable ideas or other opportunities for already highly successful individuals, families and businesses.

These advisors pass my screen tests and include estate planning attorneys, CPA's, money managers, fundraisers, investment bankers, and other financial experts. Some of my best referrers are other life insurance agents who know our best client type and can benefit from partnering with us.

You may be surprised to see life insurance agents on my list. Our team has national caliber expertise in our areas of specialty. The life agents we work with bring the client, and we bring the expertise. That's a win for everyone. You can do this same thing in your business, as joint work is a great way to leverage everyone's opportunity. Leverage your time and resources so that you can bring your best ideas and capabilities to your best clients and referral sources. I partner all the time. Sometimes I'm the person bringing the client, other times I'm the subject matter expert. It's all driven by our client's or partner's needs.

My Ideal Opportunities

It's easier to recognize your best clients and referral sources than your best opportunities. The purpose of your best opportunities is to give you access to more of your best clients and referral sources. So anything which accomplishes that qualifies as a best opportunity.

I've alluded to specific types of my best opportunities, but new ones emerge all the time that are not on this list. Identify and pursue those you can spot readily and be ready for the surprises that appear out of the blue. These can be tremendous. Some of my best opportunities are as follows:

❖ *Invitations to visit or join groups or events where my ideal clients and advisors are present in abundance,*

❖ *Speaking opportunities in my areas of expertise,*

✧ *Lectures or workshops on subjects that charge my batteries and help me move forward.*

IDENTIFYING YOUR BIG THREE

Take time to complete your own Big-Three profile now, and you will be well prepared to interview your best clients and referrers. Your chance of meeting them will skyrocket, because when you know specifically whom and what you're looking for, you become a magnet for them.

By taking the time to complete the profile, I refined my vision when I began to think in terms of my Big Three. I wanted to work not only with people whom I liked, trusted and respected, but also with those who charged my batteries and could help me advance my vision of my best life going forward. My intention is to teach you how to do this for yourself and for others in order to help them, refer them and be referred by them.

We all share this in common about our vision. Either we want to do what we are presently doing better, or we want to do something else entirely. Or perhaps it's somewhere in between. Whatever it is that motivates us, improving what we are currently doing will get us to our goal sooner. The most efficient way to enhance our current business is to meet more of our very best clients and referrers.

As you complete your own profile, begin with your vision and identify your Big Three with that vision in mind. When you have done this for yourself, you will be able to do this for others, and you will move towards your dream by helping them achieve theirs.

The profile that follows lists some of my favorite questions. You may also download it from my blog at HankFrazee.com. I've included plenty of questions to add flexibility and allow you to pick and choose which questions are most appropriate for your own vision, style and business. The questions are listed by category as business and personal. You can choose to complete only those questions that will best identify your Big Three to your potential referrers and delete those questions that don't apply to you. You're creating the first draft of your own profile which, with some improvements, you will later share with your best clients and referrers.

BIG-THREE PROFILE FOR:

Name: _____ **Date:** _____

Business

*What do you do for a living?*_____

_____

_____

How did you get started in your line of work? _____

_____

_____

*Describe your best types of clients:*_____

_____

_____

What do you do for your very best clients? _____

_____

_____

Describe your best types of referrers: _____

_____

_____

Whom would you like to meet, specifically or generally?

_____

_____

_____

What do you see as your best opportunities to grow your business? _____

_____

_____

How do you meet new clients and referrers? _____

_____

_____

What groups or organizations attract your Big Three (your best clients, referrers and opportunities)? _____

_____

_____

What activities might give you greater access to your Big Three? _____

_____

_____

What might someone say that would indicate to me that this is someone you should meet? _____

_____

_____

_____

If you weren't doing this, what would you love to do?

_____

_____

_____

Personal

What is your vision of your best life going forward? _____

_____

_____

_____

_____

Do you play golf or other sports? _____

_____

_____

Who are your current advisors? _____

_____

_____

_____

Which of your advisors would you recommend and why?

_____

_____

_____

Tell me about yourself, your family, and your interests:

_____

_____

_____

_____

_____

What are your favorite charities? _____

_____

_____

_____

Where did you grow up? _____

_____

Where did you go to school? _____

_____

What is important to you? _____

_____

_____

_____

_____

What are you most proud of? _____   _____

_____

_____

_____

_____

What are your hobbies and social, civic and charitable interests? _____

_____

_____

_____

If we were sitting here three years from today, looking back to today, what has to happen for you to feel happy personally and professionally? * _____

_____

_____

_____

_____

_____

_____

What are your top three dangers, opportunities and strengths? * _____

_____

_____

_____

_____

_____

_____

_____

*Questions with an asterisk are from Dan Sullivan at The Strategic Coach®.

7

PERSISTENCE

*"There is nothing impossible
to him who will try."*

ALEXANDER THE GREAT

I'VE NOTICED THIS ABOUT NEARLY EVERYONE, including myself. We allow ourselves to be distracted by our own negative self-talk. The best way I've found to check this tendency is to continually bring my mind back to my vision and take action steps to realize it. Overcoming negative thinking is much like bringing your thoughts back to the mantra when your mind wanders in meditation. Bring your mind back to your vision and take a specific step towards making it happen. You can wait until you quit telling yourself all the reasons you can't do this or that it won't work, or you can just go ahead and do it anyway. Let me encourage you to forge ahead, in spite of the ongoing blather from the critic in your head.

All of the mental obstacles discussed in this chapter can be overcome by repeatedly bringing your attention back to your vision and by taking action to realize it. It can be done, and you can do it. I know that is so, because there are countless people in your industry and mine who are achieving tremendous success. They are having their best year ever. Those who are succeeding are either helping greater numbers of clients, or they are helping bigger clients. Isn't it time you joined them? It's time to take advantage of your opportunities, and you can do that by helping others to reach their goals. It's that simple. There is a reason God didn't put each of us on our own little planet. We are here to help one another.

So let's break through the fears and obstacles. Pick up the phone, get educated, or take whatever step you can at the moment. If you'd like to shorten your learning curve, partner up. When you do joint work, your chances of getting the deal, and the size of the deal, both increase exponentially. Partnering is often one of the quickest routes to improving your results, and it enables you to bring the best possible resources to the client.

Review this chapter if you start doing a mind trip on yourself as your progress. But again, the key is to return to your vision, keep taking action steps towards it, and success will be yours.

MENTAL ROADBLOCKS AND SOLUTIONS

✧ *I can't do it.*

Yes, you can! It doesn't matter if you've been in business 30 days or 30 years. It can be done. I am doing it, and so can anyone who applies the concepts in this book.

✧ *I don't know how to do it.*

Read and reread this book and take action. Taking action to advance your goal is the key to succeeding.

✧ *I don't know anyone.*

Increase your access to opportunity. Join a club with an emphasis on an activity you love, such as golf or tennis. Get active in your faith community. Get on the board of a charity or civic group or school that you care about. Volunteer where there are people you'd like to meet. Call your existing or prospective clients and referral sources using the methods described in the next chapter.

✧ *I have the expertise but don't have the contacts.*

Partner with someone who is a good rainmaker and has an abundance of contacts. He or she is likely looking for someone like you.

✧ *I have the contacts but don't have the expertise.*

There are three sure-fire ways to gain expertise, through study, individual experience and joint work with someone who has the experience and expertise you're still developing. Form or join a study group, get credentials, attend your industry events, and you will advance in your knowledge and experience.

✧ *I'm afraid to ask them to dance.*

Ask them anyhow, and if you don't want to dance with them, invite them to dance with your partner. Discipline yourself to ask 25 people per day, and you will overcome your fear.

✧ *I haven't identified my Big Three.*

Do it now. Then take the action steps suggested in the following chapters, and you will find your Big Three.

✧ *It takes too much time.*

Is there a shorter path to exponentially increase your access to your Big Three?

✧ *I don't have good people skills.*

Take a course that addresses the specific areas you want to improve.

✧ *I don't look good.*

Consult a makeover specialist.

✧ *Nobody likes me.*

If you follow the instructions in this book and continue to take action steps towards your goal, this will take care of itself. It's challenging to try something new, especially if we are beating up on ourselves along the way. You can do this, and you have a right to make your life better. Focus on what you want and embrace your vision of a better future. Hold onto that vision, take the steps in front of you, and you will make it.

8

GET THE APPOINTMENT

*"The difference between the right word
and the almost right word is the difference
between lightning and a lightning bug."*

MARK TWAIN

NOW THAT YOU'VE IDENTIFIED YOUR BIG Three and know how to overcome your obstacles, it's time to make some appointments. When I began in business, I noticed three things.

✧ *Those who made phone calls got appointments.*

✧ *Those who got appointments placed business.*

✧ *Those who placed business got paid.*

Naturally, I wanted to be among those who got paid, and it didn't take me long to realize that the more calls I made, the more people I saw, the more money I made.

So I decided to devote from nine to eleven each morning to making phone calls to book appointments. That worked well. So I reasoned that if I moved all the activity that didn't involve seeing people to Fridays, it might work even better. Then I came up with the nine-to-four rule, which meant that between nine and four, Monday through Thursday, I had just two objectives in mind—meeting with a prospect or calling to make appointments. Back then, I made sixty-two phone calls each day for years. I kept records, and my business flourished. I don't need to make that many calls now, but doing so definitely works when you are new in business.

Most people resist calling for appointments for several reasons:

✧ *They are afraid of rejection.*

✧ *They don't like being screened by the receptionist, or turned down by the client if they do get through.*

✧ *They may invest valuable time for minimal results.*

What if there was an easier way? There is. Let's look at two methods that will transform your business completely *if* you put them to work for you.

REFERRAL SOURCE PHONE SCRIPT

Let's say I'm calling John Abacus, an accountant I know who may have clients that match my best client profile. When I dial his number, his assistant will answer:

"Good Morning, this is the accounting office of John Abacus, how may I help you?"

HANK: *"Good morning, this is Hank Frazee, may I speak with John?"*

ASSISTANT: *"May I ask what this is about?"*

HANK: *"Yes, tell him I want to speak to him about referring him."*

John will get on the phone. Or, if he is busy, his assistant may offer to put me through to his voicemail. I will say yes and leave the message as stated above and my number. That is the entire script. He will call back. Back when I was making dozens of phone calls each day, I devised numerous scripts with multiple questions to get to the key question that would get the appointment. This works better.

Let's pause for a moment. The essence of what happened in the above call is that I focused on what I could do to help John. That is a powerful mind shift. It changes the dynamics completely, for both parties. When you focus on what you can do to help your prospect, his attitude towards you changes and he will agree to meeting with you. It bears repeating that you must sincerely wish to refer him. But you are offering much more than just a referral. You are offering to help him achieve his dreams. And when he understands that, he will love you.

Let me give you another example. For over a year, I had been trying to meet with a potential referrer. Let's call him Pete Stuart, the managing partner of a major law firm. Though we had a friendly acquaintance, we've spoken only occasionally in the last few years. For months, I tried to get in front of him, and for many months nothing worked. I put my assistant on it, with the same results. We tried email, still nothing. We asked another of our partners to book the appointment with a partner in the firm. We advanced only part way up the ladder.

Pete has numerous billionaire clients and even more in the hundred-million-up category, so showing him what we could do would be a big deal. But we never succeeded in securing the appointment. That's because he knew all along that it was all about me, rather than about him, and how I might use him to get to his clients. I'm putting it bluntly for a reason. We must be clear that this is how we come across to the people we call about showing them our products and services. We must acknowledge this in order to change it.

So I changed my mindset and my method, with the following results. As an experiment, I asked my assistant, Eileen, to call using this two-sentence script. Here is the call exactly as it went:

PETE'S ASSISTANT: *"Pete Stuart's office, how may I help you?"*

EILEEN: *"Hi, this is Eileen from Hank Frazee's office. Hank would like to get together with Pete to talk about how Hank might be able to refer him."*

PETE'S ASSISTANT: *"He's on the phone, may I take a message?"*

EILEEN: *"Yes, Hank asked me to call to set up a time to get together with Pete to talk about how Hank might be able to refer him."*

PETE'S ASSISTANT: *"May I call you back?"*

EILEEN: *"Yes."*

PETE'S ASSISTANT: *"Ok, I will talk with him and call you back."*

EILEEN: *"Thanks."*

PETE'S ASSISTANT: *"Thank you."*

An hour later, Pete's assistant called back and booked the appointment. That was after a year of trying to book the appointment the old way. Do this with the hidden intention of just pitching them, and you will be toast. Do this with the genuine intention of referring them, and you will be on your way to meeting your Big Three.

Once you try this, you will abandon flying standby when it comes to getting referrals. This is so much better than making sixty-two blind calls a day and asking unproductive whom-do-you-know-who questions. This is the path to making that transition.

Delegate making appointments. This will free up your nine-to-four time significantly. Enlisting your part- or full-time or even virtual assistant to make this call is an amazingly efficient way to fill your schedule with exactly the people you need to see.

An Alternative Method

Here is a more conversational approach to making an appointment with a referral source you know socially. You may use this method or the one above on the phone or in person.

A good ice breaker is: "How did you get started in your business?" This is most always a fascinating story to hear. Be genuinely interested in hearing it.

And if it feels right, you might ask, "Are there specific people or categories of people that you would like to meet?" Again, listen attentively to the answer. And you might follow up with something like, "We seem to work with some of the same types of people. Let's get together for lunch, as I may be able to refer you."

What you say precisely is dependent on the situation and the person, of course. People are infinitely interesting if you ask them the right questions. Keep an open mind, and you'll find the words that are right for you.

Existing Client Phone Script

This call is as easy to make as the referral source call because your intention is to provide service to your existing client. Your mindset in all of these approaches, again, is giving, rather than self-promotion or selling. When you provide service before selling, the chances of making a sale are much greater.

If you've been in business for some time, you are likely an expert at getting in front of your existing clients. So bear with me as the next couple of paragraphs are aimed at the reader who is newer in his or her career.

How much actual face-to-face service do you think the average client receives each year? It's very little, because the average salesperson is off trying to sell someone else something else. Why isn't he back with his existing client providing great service and value after the sale? Isn't that the person most likely to do repeat business with him and to refer him?

We can be tempted in our hurry to reach our goals to allow undirected activity to take over, rather than planning exactly whom we will see and what we will say.

Don't ignore your existing clients. They already like, trust and respect you, or they wouldn't have bought from you in the first place. The good news is that we can go back now and conduct the Big-Three interview with our existing clients.

So how do you get in front of the existing clients you do want to see? Simple. Make it an autopilot project, meaning that you plan it, improve it and give input along the way, but allow someone else to be in charge of it. Remember, these are your clients. They will likely say yes to an invitation from you. Invite them by email or letter, and have your assistant call to schedule the date. Here is the script:

> EILEEN: *"Hello Mr. Smith, this is Eileen from Hank Frazee's office. Is this a good time to talk? I am calling regarding the email [letter] Hank sent to you about going out to lunch to catch up and say thanks for your business. When would be good for you in the next week or two?"*

Your existing clients want to see you, if you have been active with them, and will agree to meet you. Notice that your only time in this process is creating the original letter, choosing whom to go to lunch with and showing up to the appointment. If you know them well, you won't even need the letter.

The Big-Three interview may fit within the service interview, if the service interview is brief. That has been my experience. But be sure to plan for an hour and a half, if you are going to combine the Big-Three interview with a service interview.

Be selective about whom you interview, if your intention is solely to go after your Big Three. But if you are also interested in "bread and butter" referrals, you may conduct the interview with just about anyone.

As an aside, you might consider bringing your client a gift when you see him, though taking him to lunch may be sufficient. I often give a copy of my first book, *Before We Say "Goodnight" How to tell bedtime stories about your life and family*. Any gift that acknowledges who he is and what's important to him will make a difference in your relationship.

Cultivate your relationship with your existing clients, as they may refer you much more business than they personally can ever do with you. They can become your greatest friends and champions. Remember, people refer only those they like, trust and respect. Your existing clients have already bought from you and are likely to do so again. They will refer you, again and again, if you interview them and focus on helping them to reach their highest goals.

9

THE BIG-THREE
INTERVIEW

"Focus and keep it simple."

STEVE JOBS

L ET'S DISCUSS FOUR BASIC METHODS OF meeting with clients and referrers.

The Sales Interview, in which we interview our client to understand his needs with the intention of solving those needs with our product or service. Sometimes this method is used simply as a sales pitch, with no interview.

The Service Interview, in which we make sure that our product or service is working well for our client.

The Standby Referral Interview, in which our primary purpose is to ask our client or potential referrer to refer us to someone who can use our product or service.

The Relationship-Building Opportunity (RBO), in which we build relationship with our potential or existing client or referrer through activities such as golf, meals, social, business, civic, charitable events or any number of other experiences.

And then there's this old favorite, the Sales-Service-Social-Referral Interview, in which we try to cram all of the above into one all-purpose meeting. I've used this technique many times. Can we agree that this method doesn't work very well?

If we replace the Standby Referral interview with the Big-Three interview and mix up the order a bit, the list might look like this:

❖ *The Relationship-Building Opportunity*

❖ *The Big-Three Interview*

❖ *The Sales Interview*

❖ *The Service Interview*

Why conduct the interviews in this order? When you have a relationship-building experience with a potential client or referrer, you create an opportunity to build your relationship and trust prior to doing business. And building trust is key to his doing business with you and referring you to your Big Three.

I meet many people who eventually become my best clients through referrals that originated from social, golf, charitable, and business activities. These are relationship-building opportunities, as mentioned above. If you are in a business, club, civic or charitable organization, these opportunities present themselves all the time. Your RBOs are unique to you and your life, so they won't be the same as mine, but they are there if you look for them. RBOs can occur in personal rather than professional contexts as well, at school or sports functions, hobbies or other social experiences.

When you have created some relationship through an RBO, the next step is to schedule the Big-Three interview. If you are face-to-face with your client or referrer, you might say, "Let's get together for lunch. I think I may be able to refer you." You will already have learned about his profession through your relationship-building experience and whether he could be someone whom you could introduce to his Big Three. Granted, you may get quicker results heading straight for the sales interview, but you might also end up having a one-and-done experience with no sale and no referral to your Big Three.

A good rule-of-thumb is the bigger the opportunity, the longer the lead-time. Consider modifying your current method for one with much bigger promise and fulfillment. You don't have to conduct the Big-Three interview with every client and referrer that you know, be selective. You will likely want to interview just your very best prospective clients or referrers.

Conducting the Big Three interview will save you a great deal of time. Think about it. Plenty of people look like they could be a wonderful referral source for you. The catch is that you cannot tell if they are or not, during a normal sales interview. The idea is to avoid spending the rest of our careers chasing people who may never refer us to anyone. I spent years doing that myself. You'll find this out fairly quickly in your Big-Three interviews, and that is actually a great blessing.

Take all that time that would have been wasted and invest it in relationships that will be fruitful for both you and your Big Threes. It's a win-win since they will refer you over and over again, because you are continually introducing them to their Big Three. You have found the needle in the haystack. These are the people with whom you can develop a partnering relationship that can be mutually beneficial for years to come.

The primary difference between the sales and Big-Three interviews is our intention in conducting them and the results that follow from that intention. In the sales interview, we are focused on discovering our client's problem or need through an interview or analytical method and providing a solution with our product or service.

In the Big-Three interview, the client is generally non-defensive and open in his answers as he quickly realizes we aren't trying to sell him anything. This puts you in an excellent position when you do transition into the sales interview or brainstorming session, as you will have built trust and understand more thoroughly your client's needs.

Likewise, the Big-Three interview gives you a much better platform to secure referrals from your other potential referral sources. The old method of getting a referral from non-client referral sources usually goes something like this: you pitch your product or service to them in the hope that they will be inspired to introduce you to a prospect. In the Big Three referrer interview, by contrast, you are focused on their vision of their best life going forward and helping them get there. You differentiate yourself from every other salesperson. They, in turn, will want to know how they can help you to reach your dreams. I experience this nearly every day, and so can you. This is a completely new way of approaching and relating to your referral sources, and the results will speak for themselves.

Of course, it's not always feasible to conduct the interviews in the order listed above, nor will you want to. You may be referred to someone who needs a product or service immediately, and it makes sense to proceed to the sales interview without the Big-Three interview or a relationship-building opportunity. In those instances, you may want to ask a few key questions from the Big-Three profile, as this will help you to get to know the potential client more quickly. Some of my favorites are:

✧ *Describe your best types of clients.*

✧ *What do you do for your very best clients?*

✧ *Describe your best types of referrers.*

✧ *What do you see as your best opportunities to grow your business?*

✧ *What groups or organizations attract your Big Three (your best clients, referrers and opportunities)?*

THE BIG-THREE REFERRER INTERVIEW

You, or your assistant, have scheduled the appointment with your potential referrer. Let's assume this appointment is with someone that you know fairly well. The other possibility is that you have been referred to him by someone you like, trust and respect, such as another client or referrer.

Begin your interview with a brief reminder of why you are there, namely that you would like to interview him because you think you might be able to refer him. Feel free to modify the language in any way that fits you.

"Bill, I mentioned that I might be able to refer you. I'd like to interview you to determine whom you would like to meet specifically and by category. When we're done, I'll have your profile, which I can use on an on-going basis to more easily introduce you to your ideal clients, referral sources and opportunities, what I call your Big Three. This can become a good tool for you to use as well to find your ideal clients, referral sources and opportunities. You can share your profile with as many people as you would like who also may be able to introduce you."

Following these comments, you will interview your potential referrer by asking him ten to twelve questions from the Big-Three profile. The interview is conducted entirely from the profile. You can use the profile in its original format or customize it in any way you like. There are more than ten to twelve questions in the profile, found at the end Chapter 10, to give you flexibility with the direction you want to take the interview. Sample profiles are available at HankFrazee.com.

For the sake of simplicity, I am going to assume that you know your potential referrer at least a little. Notice that the first question in the interview is, "What do you do for a living?" I ask that question even when I am certain of the answer, as it puts him at ease. He knows this one. He also gets into the frame of mind that he is being interviewed, and his answers often will be more specific than in casual conversation. You will learn more about him, and it sets up his willingness to answer the rest of the questions thoughtfully.

It can take an hour easily to complete the interview with a good potential referrer. I try to limit my appointments to an hour or so, as that is what most people allow for and it's meant to be fun, not fatiguing. You can always add information to the profile in subsequent interviews.

By the end of the interview, you may have someone in mind that you can introduce him to immediately. Since you are interviewing a potential referrer, as opposed to a client, the next meeting will be an introduction by you to one of his Big Three. Attend that first meeting, as your presence will demonstrate your commitment to helping them both to connect with each other. If you cannot come up with a referral for him in your first meeting, you may have the opportunity to schedule a follow-up interview, also referred to as a brainstorming session, to explore how you might work together to introduce each other.

How will you know if you should schedule a follow-up? If your potential referrer is excited about the interview and intrigued by the prospect of providing mutual referrals, proceed to book the follow-up. If he is not particularly excited, you may choose to refer him or you may decide that this may not be the right person for you. On the other hand, you are there to discover how best to refer him, and you may find in doing so that he will warm up to the idea of referring you as well. That is a call you will make, though it should be fairly easy if you've been focusing on him and paying close attention.

A Hidden Opportunity With Referrers

When you interview those who are already among your best referrers, be sure to ask them specifically about their best advisors in a specific category you are interested in, such as accountants or attorneys. If they are unflattering of their own advisors or don't have anyone in a category in which you have someone who's terrific, you have an instant opportunity to make a favorable introduction. Or if they are highly complementary about a specific advisor, make note as this can be an advisor you may have the opportunity to be introduced to later. Be careful that you do not come across like you're trying to bypass him to gain access to his advisiors, who may be his highly valued referral sources. Remember your focus is to refer *him* and stay in interview mode.

When you are referred to potential clients and referrers, interview them as well. You will make a strong positive impression if you begin your first meeting with a new potential referrer completely focused on him, his vision and whom you can introduce him to in order to realize his dream. He will be pleasantly surprised as he likely anticipated your coming at him with a sales pitch. Isn't that precisely why you resist meeting people who are referred to you? Instead, by interviewing him and offering to help him, you will build your relationship and his trust in you. He will be much more likely to want your product or service, and refer you, and you will know how to better serve him by having interviewed him first.

INTERVIEWING YOUR STRATEGIC PARTNERS

In my business, joint work with other advisors is very common. For me, strategic partners are advisors with whom I share revenue. To recap, we provide the idea or expertise, while our strategic partners bring the client or referral source. You may have similar alliances in your business, so I encourage you to interview your strategic partners as well. You will learn amazing things about them, and, in sharing your profiles, you will have a much better idea of the opportunities you can bring to one another.

THE BIG-THREE CLIENT INTERVIEW

The Big-Three client interview is similar to the Big-Three referrer interview. I begin by telling new or existing clients that the way I look at it, my job is to help other people get what they want. With that in mind, I would like to interview them to learn how I can serve them best.

Proceed by asking your client ten to twelve questions from the Big-Three profile. You will find out what your client really wants to achieve in life and who and what can help him to achieve those goals. Try to limit these interviews to about an hour. You can always add information to the profile in subsequent interviews. If you do run out of time, you may suggest to your client that you continue the interview the next day on the phone for the last few questions. This demonstrates your interest in him and commitment to follow through and also allows for a natural transition to the next steps, such as scheduling an introduction or sales interview.

If your prospective client is retired, perhaps he needs help finding his Big Two, his ideal advisors and his ideal opportunities. It is likely that at least part of his vision remains unfulfilled, and you can help him to move it forward. This kind of service truly sets you apart in your client's mind. Retired clients may be interested also in meeting or introducing others in their former industry. For example, if they played a significant role in their industry community, they may have numerous contacts who might appreciate meeting you.

The first several questions in the profile are aimed specifically at clients who are in business. But these questions can be a great way to build relationship with your retired clients and reveal hidden referral possibilities when you ask the questions in the past tense. For example, "Who were your best clients when you were in business?" Your retired client may be more likely to refer you, as he may have less concern about protecting ongoing business relationships. Experiment and find what works best for you.

A HIDDEN OPPORTUNITY WITH BIG-THREE CLIENTS

As in your referrer interviews, ask your clients about their current advisors one by one, in detail. Your clients may be happy with some of their advisors and unhappy with others, or may have gaps in their advisor team. Ask them what they like and don't like about their current service and whom they would recommend.

This is a wonderful opportunity to help your clients improve the quality of their team. You may want to meet the advisors they love and offer to replace the ones they don't. This works for nearly everyone, as most people want the best advisors they can find. On the other hand, resist any urge to push if they want to stay with a particular advisor, even one they complain about.

Your clients will eagerly refer you to the advisors they like, as it is nonthreatening and gives them another chance to vet you through professionals that have already passed their Buffet test.

Notice that you have just been referred by your mutual client to another of his or her advisors. This is a big opportunity that most people overlook and is a great starting place for an introduction. When you focus on this part of the interview, you can be referred in nearly every client interview to other advisors who share a

Big-Three client in common with you. When you interview these new advisors, your chances of being referred to more of your Big Three multiply.

When you have completed the interview, tell your clients that you will email them a copy of their Big-Three profile. You are helping them to take greater charge of their own future, and you'll be able to introduce them to others who can also help them get where they want to go. Your clients will feel valued by you, and you will score high on their screen tests. Follow through with introducing them to their Big Two or Three, and they will introduce you to yours.

At the end of the meeting, you have the opportunity to share your own profile with them, and, perhaps now more than ever, they will understand precisely what you do and the type of client you are looking for. The likelihood of your being referred will improve accordingly. They will be more likely to buy your products or services as well, as their understanding of what you do will have increased in the process. I've had that nice surprise happen frequently during the interview.

A FEW KEY POINTS TO REMEMBER

In any interview, my greatest temptation is the urge to interrupt or become conversational. Resist doing this. Be as conversational as you like before and after but not during the interview. The more you allow them to respond without interruption, the more you'll hear their vision and the greater your chance of truly understanding and connecting with them. Even when they ask questions about my work in the course of the interview, and it's tempting to go into conversation mode, experience has taught me to steer the interview back in their direction.

If you think of something to say or someone to refer them to during the interview, just make note of it on their profile. You will make more of an impact telling them your thoughts after the interview, rather than interrupting the flow, though it's fine to ask clarifying questions.

Generally, this is a one-on-one experience, but it can work as two- or even three-on-one if you don't bombard them with questions. Decide in advance who will ask the questions and who will take notes. You can interview a couple at the same time as well.

Clients and referrers gradually let their guard down and appreciate the interview process when they realize that you are there to learn about them, rather than to sell yourself and your products or services or pound them for referrals.

10

THE BIG-THREE PROFILE

"It takes reason to answer a question well.
It takes imagination to ask it well."

ANONYMOUS

YOUR BEST CLIENTS, REFERRAL SOURCES AND
opportunities will be revealed to you when you
have completed your own Big-Three profile. This is a
crucial step in making your own vision crystal clear,
and it will also serve as the road map for your clients
and referrers to introduce you to your Big Three. Based
on the information in your profile, they may suggest
ideas or opportunities that you've never considered.
Opportunities come in many shapes and sizes, yet they
all have one thing in common. They increase your access
to your best clients.

Be sure to complete your own profile prior to your first Big-Three interview. Take time to really think about your own vision and who specifically and by category you want to meet and what opportunities might help you get there. This will refine and strengthen your own vision and will enable you and your potential referrers to recognize your Big Three when you and they encounter them.

THE BIG-THREE PROFILE

The Big-Three profile is designed to identify and record the Big Threes of your clients and referrers. You may customize it to fit your industry or business. It provides a quick reference to make introductions now and in the future. And it creates an opening for you to share your own Big-Three profile, because you will bring it with you to the interview.

The questions are designed to draw out the individuals whom you interview, encouraging them to think about and share their vision. Most clients and referrers appreciate this kind of attention, which is a good sign that you are on the right track. Naturally, no one will answer these questions the same way. If they trust you, they will be open in their answers, as the questions are nonthreatening. The interview will foster a closer relationship and will increase the chances of their meeting with you again.

Some of your clients and referrers may introduce you right away as a result of your interviewing them. You also may have the opportunity to introduce them immediately or to proceed to a follow-up session to strategize how you can introduce each other in the future. The more valued the prospective client or referrer, the more you will want to prove yourself by referring him to his Big Three before moving into a sales or follow-up interview. This will be a choice you make case by case.

Occasionally reviewing the profiles of those you have interviewed, especially prior to conducting a new interview, will keep them fresh in your mind and will greatly increase your likelihood of making and receiving referrals. I have found reviewing their profile prior to a follow-up appointment to be a very useful practice.

Bring a copy of your Big-Three profile with you to your interviews, so that your interviewee will have a written record of your vision and exactly whom you'd like to meet. You are the director of how you want your clients and referrers to perceive you, your vision and your Big Three. Make your profile engaging and make it count.

THE BIG-THREE PROFILE QUESTIONS

All the questions have the following intentions: to understand his vision and help him bring it into reality, and to identify and introduce your client or referrer to his Big Three, as the shortest path to his success. Be alert to whom and what you have in common as another way to deepen your connectivity. By introducing him to his Big Three, you create a terrific recipe for ongoing reciprocal introductions.

Your profile may distinguish you as a great referrer and resource, whereas his profile may identify him as a best client or referrer. In the process, you may discover that you fit well together and have immense potential to help each other. This upgrades your own thinking as well, namely that you are an ideal referrer for someone, maybe this someone and hopefully for many others as well.

Though the questions are listed by category as business and personal, ask them in whatever order is most comfortable for you. You may choose to change the order around, based on how the interview progresses. Generally, it makes sense to begin by asking easy questions at first and proceeding to more complex questions as you go along. For instance, you might ask about his vision a bit further into the interview, but I've done it the other way around too. As long as he understands that the purpose of this interview is to refer him, it will turn out well.

Once you have completed asking the questions, briefly tell your client or referrer what you heard him say. He will be anticipating your feedback, and you want to acknowledge him for having shared his story. Remain truly interested. Providing positive feedback about his answers and his vision is a significant part of this process. Amend any areas of his profile that may seem unclear. The more genuinely interested you are, as you review the profile with him, the more likely you will be seen as a valuable resource and friend.

This is a good time to suggest a referral if you have one. Remember, referring him to his bread-and-butter opportunities provides terrific value also. These are people that aren't necessarily his Big Three, but can be beneficial to him.

When you give him your profile, he may give you referrals right then. Don't be concerned if this doesn't happen. The idea is for you to refer him. So long as he is willing to be referred and to meet with you for a follow-up or brainstorming session or a sales interview, you're making progress in the right direction.

Transfer his profile into your system when you return to your office. Then email a copy to him and ask for any corrections or clarification. This further emphasizes that you are serious about introducing him to his Big Three. Tell him you will keep a copy of his profile for reference and that you will be on the lookout for people you can refer to him as you meet with others. If you haven't done so already, schedule your next meeting with him.

When you introduce him to someone new, both will engage more fully if you attend the first meeting. You are the candle in the darkened room. Your presence strengthens the power of their connection. When you get together, arrange to pay for lunch. Get the conversation going by making a brief introduction and tell them why you thought they should meet. Then sit back a little, as you will learn much more about them by listening intently and speaking only as needed to keep the ball rolling.

In the process, you are beginning to develop your team of rainmakers and transitioning from mere salesperson to an extraordinarily valuable resource to those you serve. You are helping your clients and referrers achieve their dreams, and that generally does not happen in ordinary sales interviews.

A couple of pointers. Resist giving your interviewee six referrals all at once. If you overwhelm him with too many referrals in the first meeting, you may miss the opportunity. You want to nurture this seedling along so that it grows into a healthy tree that steadily produces Big Threes.

Don't dismay if you don't have anyone to refer to him immediately. You will find someone. You are well connected, or have partnered with someone who is. Partner the pieces you are missing to learn, earn and grow, as you move forward in your abilities. Remember to review his profile from time to time, especially before conducting other interviews, as this will increase your chances of referring him.

The interview process increases your clients' and referrers' sense of clarity about their dreams and who can help them get there. And who makes that possible? You do.

BIG-THREE PROFILE FOR:

Name: _____ Date: _____

Business

What do you do for a living? _____
_____
_____

How did you get started in your line of work? _____
_____
_____

Describe your best types of clients: _____
_____
_____

What do you do for your very best clients? _____
_____
_____

Describe your best types of referrers: _____
_____
_____

Whom would you like to meet, specifically or generally?
_____
_____
_____

*What do you see as your best opportunities to grow your business?*_____

_____

_____

How do you meet new clients and referrers? _____

_____

_____

What groups or organizations attract your Big Three (your best clients, referrers and opportunities)? _____

_____

_____

*What activities might give you greater access to your Big Three?*_____

_____

_____

What might someone say that would indicate to me that this is someone you should meet? _____

_____

_____

_____

If you weren't doing this, what would you love to do?

_____

_____

_____

Personal

What is your vision of your best life going forward? _____

_____

_____

_____

_____

Do you play golf or other sports? _____

_____

_____

Who are your current advisors? _____

_____

_____

_____

Which of your advisors would you recommend and why?

_____

_____

_____

Tell me about yourself, your family, and your interests:

_____

_____

_____

_____

_____

What are your favorite charities? _____

_____

_____

_____

Where did you grow up? _____

_____

Where did you go to school? _____

_____

What is important to you? _____

_____

_____

_____

_____

What are you most proud of? _____

_____

_____

_____

_____

*What are your hobbies and social, civic and charitable
interests?* _____

_____

_____

_____

If we were sitting here three years from today, looking back to today, what has to happen for you to feel happy personally and professionally? * _____

_____

_____

_____

_____

_____

_____

What are your top three dangers, opportunities and strengths? * _____

_____

_____

_____

_____

_____

_____

*Questions with an asterisk are from Dan Sullivan at The Strategic Coach®.

11

FOLLOW THROUGH

*"The future depends on what
we do in the present."*

MAHATMA GANDHI

YOU HAVE SUCCESSFULLY CONDUCTED YOUR
FIRST interview, and your client is interested.
That's awesome, because now you can see that this will
work and that you can do it. All you need is a track to
run on, a system of follow through, and this idea will
take you and your Big Three to the moon.

Don't expect your client or referrer to initiate the
next steps. He won't. But if you do and meet with him
and refer him, he'll pick up on the pattern and will participate in mutually referring you.

You will be referred to your Big Three if you follow through with your promises after the interview. The follow through is crucially important. I recommend that you use a Customer Relationship Management (CRM) program. There are many good ones to choose from, and some may be designed specifically for your industry. These easy-to-use programs will help you stay on top of your activity. If you don't use a system, you may forget what you promised, and your reputation will go down rather than up.

THE CHECKLIST

For ease of reference, the following is a list of all the steps in the *Referral Upgrade* process from start to finish.

✧ *Identify your Big Three using the method described in Chapter 6.*

✧ *Fill out your own Big-Three profile.*

✧ *Enter the names of the prospects you would like to interview in your CRM or other program. You and your assistant can work the list together or separately.*

✧ *Call and book the initial interview, using the scripts discussed in Chapter 8, and send a confirmation email.*

✧ *Print (or download onto your tablet) the Big-Three profile you will use in your interviews. You can customize it as you gain more experience.*

✧ *Meet with your client or referrer to conduct the interview. Remember to tell him you'd like to interview him as you think you may be able to refer him.*

✧ *Focus your attention entirely on him and his vision throughout the interview.*

✧ *Review his profile with him at the end of the interview and recap what you heard. Amend or correct anything your interviewee may suggest. Notice that this is a great opportunity to give people sincere positive feedback, and they appreciate hearing it.*

✧ *Discuss any potential referrals that may have occurred to you during the interview.*

✧ *If you have someone in mind, tell him that your assistant will contact him to schedule a date to make the introduction.*

✧ *Or, if appropriate, schedule the date now for a follow-up session in which you trade profiles and brainstorm how you can work together to introduce each other to your Big Threes.*

✧ *Or, if you sense the timing is not quite right to schedule the follow-up interview, tell him you will be on the lookout for the right person for him and follow through with referring him.*

✧ *Give him a copy of your own Big-Three profile in this first interview. Walk through it briefly, so he understands the type of people you are looking for.*

✧ *If you find out that he is someone else's ideal client rather than yours, offer to make that introduction and conclude your interview here.*

✧ *If he is in the right category of client or referrer for you, return to your office and have your assistant type up a copy of his interview profile and then proof it. This will assure the accuracy of his profile and help you to internalize his Big Three, so you will recognize them when you see them.*

✧ *Send or email a thank you note along with a copy of his profile. Reference your next action steps, such as an introduction meeting or follow-up session.*

✧ *If you have someone to refer to him and have not already done so, have your assistant schedule a face-to-face introduction, with you present, at a location convenient to your guests. Hosting breakfast or lunch works well. The idea is to build relationship with each of them, and that's easy to do if you are present to do it.*

✧ *Or if your next step is a follow-up session and it hasn't been booked yet, schedule it and be sure to have a copy of his printed profile ready in advance. Don't wait for the day of the appointment and then try to decipher your notes. Follow up with a confirming email or letter.*

✧ *Confirm the time and location of the introduction meeting the day before with both parties.*

✧ *During the introduction meeting, do a little matchmaking but mostly sit back, listen and let them get to know each other.*

✧ *Call each of them to follow up. If appropriate, set up a follow- up session with the first person to discuss creating an ongoing plan of identifying and referring him to his Big Three. Or give him another referral.*

✧ *Then schedule an interview with the second person, if you haven't done so already. These are major opportunities. It really shows both parties that you mean to continue to refer them to their best clients and referral sources. Would you like it if someone like this showed up in your life? I would, and this is the path to making that happen.*

You could manage this process easily using just this list, if you had only two prospects. But you can tell that each person you refer becomes another prospect for yet another interview and brainstorming session. And whomever they refer to you becomes a prospect, and so on. When it becomes wildly successful, you will need a CRM system to handle it. That's a good thing, because soon, if you choose to, this could become the basis for most of your calls and prospecting. And the people you meet will become either your best clients or referral sources, and, before you know it, you will be swimming in a sea of Big Threes.

BRAINSTORMING SESSIONS

The initial brainstorming session is a chance for you and your client or referrer to begin working together. Meeting in person gives you a greater chance to bond since only ten percent of communication is through what we say, but you can do the session over the phone if that is the way it works out. During the session, show your interviewee how to identify his Big Three and how to interview others if he's interested in doing so. To facilitate that, give him a sample copy of the Big-Three profile.

Take it slowly and let him warm up to you and the idea. If it works out well, the initial brainstorming session can be the foundation of your ongoing plan of actively referring each other.

Once you have done a few interviews, you will have the hang of it and, deep down, you will know the following:

✧ *The Big-Three interview strengthens your relationship and changes your status with your prospects from salesperson to invaluable resource.*

✧ *Your clients and referrers view you as someone who is helping them achieve their dreams.*

✧ *They trust you.*

✧ *They want to help you to meet your Big Three, partly out of a sense of reciprocity, but also because they know that introducing you makes you more likely to continue introducing them to their Big Three.*

✧ *This works!*

Best of all, you have created a system which will facilitate your being introduced continually to your very best clients, referrers and opportunities by introducing others to theirs.

12

YOUR TEAM OF RAINMAKERS

*"The people who get on in this world are the people
who get up and look for circumstances they want
and if they can't find them, make them."*

GEORGE BERNARD SHAW

IN THIS CHAPTER, WE'LL TAKE *Referral Upgrade*
to the next logical level. But first, let's review how far
we've come.

You have taken the significant step of identifying
your Big Three. Using the screen tests, you are being far
more selective in your choice of potential prospects or
clients. You are conducting interviews and brainstorming sessions with your most promising prospects and
turning those relationships into ongoing referrals for

each other. In other words, you are making the highest and best use of your time and spending more and more of it with people you really enjoy. Your work and the people in it are charging your batteries. Your access to opportunity is growing. And you are using a system and keeping records on a CRM, so that your hard work and good intentions aren't falling through the cracks.

In keeping with your giving mindset, you are focusing on truly helping your interviewees to live their dreams by introducing them to their Big Three. And you know, from experience now, that this inevitably leads to introductions to your Big Three. You are giving and receiving introductions of consequence. As you progress, you realize that this is becoming so successful that you have become more selective about whom you interview.

So, how would you like to take this to another level? Imagine building a strong team of referrers, strategic partners and champions who are constantly introducing you to your Big Three. It can be done. I am doing it, and so can you. You'll experience exciting possibilities that are much more promising than anything you've encountered so far in conducting only sales and service interviews. And here's the way to make that happen.

Step 1—Teach Your Big Three to Conduct Their Own Interviews

Working with your referrers individually is good, but encouraging them to conduct their own interviews is even more powerful. When your referrers conduct their own interviews using this process, you significantly increase your leverage and access to opportunity. By empowering them with these tools, you automatically evolve into one of their Big Three, and they will actively refer you.

Step 2—Introduce Them to One Another

You have the opportunity to create a group of people consciously seeking to help others to live their dreams, and that can't help but flow back to referrals for you. I am happy to tell you that I've seen this proven over and over again.

Introducing your Big-Three referrers to one another can create mutual referrals among all of you, which will increase your level of success and access to opportunity even further. Imagine your team of rainmakers, a group of interrelated, influential referrers continually making Big-Three referrals to one another as a part of their daily routine.

You will be the founding member of your team, and each member will think the world of you for including him or her. Share your profiles and supercharge your team efforts, as you continually promote, assist and refer one another.

Step 3—Invite Them to Participate in Relationship-Building Opportunities Together

An excellent way of deepening your connection with your team individually and collectively is to gather them together periodically, which will strengthen friendships and increase the chances of everyone mutually referring one another. Golf, dinner including your significant others, and travel opportunities are just a few examples of great bonding experiences. The list of RBOs is endless and will flow from the recreational pursuits and interests of the individual members on your team. Remember to follow only those suggestions that charge your batteries.

In summary, you can create your team of rainmakers in three simple steps:

✧ *Teach your Big Three who particularly resonate with these ideas to conduct their own interviews.*

✧ *Introduce them to one another for mutual referral opportunities.*

✧ *Invite them collectively to relationship-building opportunities which can deepen their connectivity.*

Introducing your Big Three to one another will greatly expand your access to opportunity. As you connect and deepen these relationships, your batteries will be charged by the abundance of referrals you give and receive from your team of rainmakers. And, as promised at the beginning of this book, you will have traded too few referrals to just anyone for as many referrals as you would like to your Big Three.

AFTERWORD

"What lies behind us and what lies before us are small matters compared to what lies within us."

RALPH WALDO EMERSON

I WISH YOU GREAT SUCCESS ON THIS journey to living your best life going forward. This book is the story of how I refined my own vision and expanded my business, and I know it will work for you as it has for me. If you plant good seeds and nurture them, your business and personal life will blossom and thrive.

At lunch one day, I suggested this method to a good friend who is the top rainmaker for a national trust company. His initial response was skeptical, "Sounds too good to be true." But as we continued to discuss the possibilities more thoroughly, he suddenly said, "This is for me!"

Right then and there, he invited me to speak on this subject at his Trusted Advisor Retreat, to be held a couple of months later. When I called him a week or so before the event, I realized that we hadn't spoken since our lunch meeting. His very first words were, "Oh my gosh, I've been interviewing people, and I had to stop!" I asked why. He said, "I'm getting too many referrals!" He has since resumed interviewing with an effective system to handle the volume.

Refine your vision of what you want to achieve and with whom you want to work. Put this process to the test and prove it for yourself. You truly have greatness within you, and it will be revealed when you put others first.

GLOSSARY OF TERMS AND CONCEPTS

ACCESS-TO-OPPORTUNITY TEST: *ideally, opportunities will pass the Buffet and the battery tests and will lead to more opportunities to meet your Big Three. The more of your personal time and effort they require, the more true this should be. Use these standards as you consider whether to join a club, charity, or any organization, whether for business or pleasure.*

BATTERY TEST: *a method to determine whether to do something or not. Ask yourself, "Does it charge my batteries, or does it drain them?" If it charges them, do it; and if it drains them, don't.*

BEST CLIENT: *a client who passes the screen tests and can make use of your best skill sets, products or services and ideally introduces you to your Big Three.*

BEST OPPORTUNITY: *a place or thing that passes the screen tests and will lead you to more of your Big Three.*

BEST REFERRER: *a referrer who passes the screen tests and who steadily refers you to your Big Three.*

BIG THREE: *Your best clients, referrers and opportunities.*

THE BIG-THREE INTERVIEW: *the interview you conduct with your best clients or referrers to identify their vision and help them find their Big Three.*

THE BIG-THREE PROFILE: *the questionnaire you use in the Big-Three interview to help your clients and referrers identify their vision and discover their Big Three, also used as a road map for introductions.*

BIG-THREE REFERRER: *a client, center of influence, strategic partner, or friend who refers you to your Big Three.*

BRAINSTORMING SESSION: *an interview in which you brainstorm with your client or referrer to help each other meet your Big Threes, also referred to as a follow-up interview.*

BREAD-AND-BUTTER THREE: *referrals whom you can help using your best skill sets, yielding smaller results than those of your Big Three.*

BUFFET TEST: *my phrase for applying Warren Buffet's quotation to your potential clients and referrers, "Regardless of the numbers, I never work with anyone I don't like, trust and respect."*

CENTER OF INFLUENCE: *someone in a related industry with whom you don't share revenue and who refers you to your Big Three.*

FLYING STANDBY: *asking for referrals in a hit-and-miss manner that generally yields few or random results.*

FOLLOW-UP INTERVIEW: *an interview in which you follow up with your client or referrer to help each other meet your Big Three, also known as a brainstorming session.*

RBO: *abbreviation for relationship-building opportunity.*

RELATIONSHIP-BUILDING OPPORTUNITY: *any social, civic, business or other activity that increases your personal connection with your best clients or referrers (RBO).*

REFEREE: *the person you are referred to.*

REFERRER: *the person who refers you.*

REFERRAL UPGRADE: *a quality introduction to any of your Big Three.*

SCREEN TESTS: *three tests to help you identify your Big Three, namely, the Buffet test, the battery test, and the access-to-opportunity test.*

STRATEGIC PARTNERS: *people in your industry with whom you share revenue and who refer you to your Big Three.*

TEAM OF RAINMAKERS: *a group of referrers who actively and regularly refer one another to their Big Threes.*

Sample Questions

Please note that some of the questions overlap to provide alternate ways to ask a similar question. When interviewing a retired client or referrer, you will want to ask some of these questions in the past tense.

Business:

What do you do for a living? _____

_____

How did you get started in your line of work? _____

_____

Describe your best types of clients: _____

_____

What do you do for your very best clients? _____

_____

Describe your best types of referrers: _____

_____

Whom would you like to meet, specifically or generally?

_____

Whom would you like to meet in your business? _____

_____

What do you like best about your work? _____

_____

What do you see as your best opportunities to grow your business? _____

_____

How do you meet new clients and referrers? _____

_____

What groups or organizations attract your Big Three?

_____

What activities might give you greater access to your Big Three? _____

_____

With whom do you want to work? _____

_____

With whom don't you want to work? _____

_____

What would you like to do more of in your work or personal life? _____

_____

*If you could push a button and change three things in your business (or personal life), what would they be?*_____

_____

What might someone say that would indicate to me that this is someone you should meet? _____

_____

What do you love to do in your work? _____

_____

What would you love to do if you weren't doing this?

_____

What don't you like to do? _____

_____

If you could draw a picture of it, what would your best life going forward look like? _____

_____

*What are you best at?*_____

_____

Personal

What is your vision of your ideal life going forward? ____

_____

What are your interests outside of work? _____

_____

Do you play golf or other sports? _____

_____

What are your big dreams and who or what will help you to get there? _____

_____

What is important to you? _____

_____

What are your kids'/grandkids' interests? _____

_____

Where is your favorite place to vacation? _____

_____

Where would you like to live if you didn't live here? ____

_____

Tell me about yourself, your family, your interests, your business: _____

_____

Where did you grow up? _____

_____

Where did you go to school? _____

_____

What are you most proud of? _____

_____

What do you do for fun? _____

_____

Who are your current advisors? _____

_____

Which of your advisors would you recommend and why?

_____

*What are your hobbies and social, civic and charitable
interests?*_____

_____

What's on your bucket list? _____

_____

_____

*If we were sitting here three years from today, looking
back to today, what has to happen for you to feel happy
personally and professionally?** _____

_____

*What are your top three dangers, opportunities and
strengths?** _____

_____

*Questions with an asterisk are from Dan Sullivan at The Strategic Coach®.

Resources

Recommended reading

How I Raised Myself From Failure To Success in Selling, by Frank Bettger, the best book on selling I have ever read.

The Seven Spiritual Laws of Success: A Practical Guide to the Fulfillment of Your Dreams by Deepak Chopra, a book I've read over and over again.

Aspire, by Kevin Hall, a great read on the power of words and the immense impact we have on others.

The Go Giver, by Bob Burg and John David Mann, a wonderful story about how to develop a giving mindset.

The Big Leap, by Gay Hendricks, great advice on how to overcome your internal obstacles and live the life you are meant to live.

MOVIES

It's a Wonderful Life

A Christmas Carol, the George C. Scott version

Groundhog Day

Pay it Forward

The Secret Life of Walter Mitty, both versions.

WORKSHOPS AND EVENTS

The Genius Network: Joe Polish's exclusive group for high-achieving entrepreneurs provides useful marketing, best practices, connections, collaboration, inspiration, and access to otherwise inaccessible experts. For more information, visit: www.geniusnetwork.com.

LifeSOULutions That Work: the world's premiere personal development company helping people to discover their purpose, build their dreams, and create a life they love living. For more information about programs

that can help create your best life, please visit: www.
MaryMorrissey.com

Million Dollar Round Table (MDRT): the Premier
Association of Financial Professionals® is an interna-
tional, independent association of more than 38,000
of the world's leading life insurance and financial services professionals from more than 450 companies in 74
countries. For more information visit: www.mdrt.org

The Strategic Coach® Program was the first coaching
program exclusively for entrepreneurs and remains highly
innovative in terms of its ability to help participants make
successive quantum leaps toward increasingly greater
personal and professional goals. Strategic Coach® clients
not only significantly increase their income and free time,
they build strong, future-focused companies. For more
information on The Strategic Coach® Program, visit their
website at www.strategiccoach.com.

ACKNOWLEDGEMENTS

To my wife, liz, for your love and faith in me and my dreams, for listening to me talk endlessly about this book, for your many hours spent editing it, and for your example of love and generosity towards others, particularly our children and me, thank you.

Special thanks to all my partners and friends with whom I so enjoy working and spending time, chief among them Mark Bugli, Marc Byrnes, Amy D'Ambra, Matt Davis, Ken Fink, Barry Hacker, Bill Hawkins, Royce Imhoff, Mike Kazanjian, Ken and Ross Kilroy, Jonas Lee, Kevin Mullane, Randy Rother, Craig Tschudi, Mike Whitmore and Andy Ziskin.

To Dan Sullivan and Babs Smith and your team, especially Maureen Sullivan Garrelts, thanks for inspiring and expanding my thinking about what's possible for so many great years.

To Joe Polish, thank you for your friendship, generosity, humor and marketing genius.

To Mary Morrissey, your dream-building ideas have helped me to live the life I love, thank you.

To Kevin Hall, many thanks for your amazing soul and unwavering belief in me.

Thanks also to my longtime friends, Tim Rogan, for your editorial help, and to Scott McNatt, for your help with production of the book.

And I particularly want to thank Eileen Waughan, my longtime assistant, for your help and friendship and exemplary work ethic.

ABOUT
THE AUTHOR

H ANK FRAZEE GREW UP IN CALIFORNIA and graduated from UCLA, with a major in English Literature. An entrepreneur, he entered the life insurance business advancing to the top one percent of insurance agents in the world.

He is the president of H.W. Frazee and Company and the founder of Sycamore Canyon Publishing. He holds the designation of Chartered Life Underwriter, CLU.

The purpose of his books is to help others connect more deeply with what matters to them and live their vision with their family, friends and customers.

Hank lives in Los Angeles with his wife and three children.

Please visit:

HankFrazee.com

for more ideas on how to find your very
best clients or to book speaking engagements or
presentations for your group or organization.

⸺∞⸺

You may also connect with Hank at:
Twitter: twitter.com/hankfrazee
Facebook: facebook.com/hankfrazee
LinkedIn: linkedin.com/hankfrazee